Be an eco hero

At School

By Sue Barraclough

Photography by Chris Fairclough

SEA-TO-SEA

Mankato Collingwood London

This edition first published in 2013 by
Sea-to-Sea Publications
Distributed by Black Rabbit Books
P.O. Box 3263, Mankato, Minnesota 56002

Printed in the United States of America, North Mankato, MN

Published by arrangement with the Watts
Publishing Group Ltd, London.

Library of Congress Cataloging-in-Publication Data

Barraclough, Sue.
 Be an eco hero at school / by Sue Barraclough ; photography by Chris
Fairclough.
    p. cm. -- (Be an eco hero)
 Includes index.
 ISBN 978-1-59771-381-8 (library binding)
 1. Environmentalism--Juvenile literature. I. Title.
 GE195.5.B375 2013
 370.286--dc23
                        2011049894

Series editor: Sarah Peutrill
Art director: Jonathan Hair
Design: Big Blu Design
Illustration: Gary Swift
Photography: Chris Fairclough, unless otherwise credited

Credits: Ian Bracegirdle/istockphoto: 8. Westphalia/istockphoto:
16c. A. Wrangler/istockphoto: 13tr.

Many thanks to the children and teachers of Ashton Gate
Primary School, Bristol, UK, for their eco-ideas and help, and for
taking part in the photo shoot.

RD/6000006415/001
May 2012

Contents

Find out ways to help your planet in this book and become an eco hero like me!

Words in **bold** are in the glossary on page 28.

At School

Schools are busy places. Schools are full of people working and learning. **Energy** is used to light and heat the school and to make machines such as computers work.

Schools use lots of water and **materials** such as paper. Schools also make lots of **garbage.**

Water

Paper

Garbage

Using Less Energy

Most energy comes from burning **fossil fuels**. Finding and using fossil fuels also makes dangerous gases that are causing **climate change**. Fossil fuels will not last forever and we are using them up fast.

Be an eco hero by:

- Turning off lights in empty rooms to save energy.
- Shutting down computers and other machines when you have finished with them.
- Closing doors and windows to save heat in cold weather.

This school has eco **monitors** who check classrooms and make sure everyone remembers to turn off the lights.

Using Less Water

We need water to drink to stay alive. We use water for sinks and toilets. We use water for growing plants and for washing and cleaning. Clean, fresh water is **precious**.

Eco heroes do not waste water.

Be an eco hero by:

• Telling a teacher about dripping faucets.

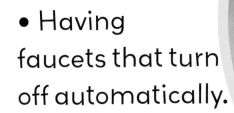

• Having faucets that turn off automatically.

SAVE WATER

• Having water-saving devices in toilets.

Busy Roads

Children and teachers need to travel to and from school almost every day. If everyone goes to school by car, this makes the roads very busy.

Busy roads are bad because:

• Cars make dangerous gases that pollute the air.

• **Pollution** can damage your health.

• Streets are dangerous and difficult to cross.

Keeping an engine running while the car is parked is highly polluting!

Cut Down Pollution

There are easy ways to cut down pollution and traffic on the roads.

Be an eco hero by:

- Sharing rides in the car.

- Walking or cycling instead of going by car.

- Helping to set up a **walking bus.**

If a school has plenty of bike racks, children are more likely to use bikes or scooters to get to school.

Walking, cycling, or scooting to school gets your brain working! It also helps to keep your body physically fit and healthy.

Garbage Problems

We are using up materials fast, so we need to use them more carefully. It is important not to **waste** materials and to throw less garbage in the trash can. Most garbage is buried in huge holes called **landfill sites**.

We are running out of space to bury garbage. So we need to **reduce**, **reuse**, and **recycle** our garbage. If every person in every school uses less, it can make a big difference.

This school has small containers for recycling food and garden waste.

Eco heroes help recycle garbage!

Reducing Garbage

Every day, we all make lots of garbage.
We throw away packages, cartons,
plastic pots, wrappers, and leftover food.

Be an eco hero by:

- Using a refillable drinks bottle.
- Using a lunchbox with sections so you do not need to wrap food.
- Choosing **recyclable** materials such as foil if you must wrap foods.
- Choosing foods with less **packaging.**

If food waste is sent to a landfill site, it breaks down without enough air. This makes dangerous gases that are a cause of climate change.

This food waste will be taken away and made into compost.

19

Reusing Things

If you reuse something, you make the best use of the time, money, energy, and materials used to make it.

This greenhouse is made from plastic bottles!

Be an eco hero by:

- Using both sides of every piece of paper.

- Reusing packaging, such as yogurt cartons and cans, for crafts and gardening.

What ways can you think of to reuse everyday objects?

21

Recycling Materials

Food, paper, glass, metal, and some plastics can be recycled. It is important to sort different materials because they are more likely to be recycled.

Paper

You can be an eco hero by sorting materials for recycling. Put materials in the correct container. Read the signs so you know which one to use.

Put fruit waste in the right container so it can be recycled.

Eco heroes sort materials for recycling!

Green and Growing

You can be an eco hero by growing your own vegetables at school. Growing plants is fun to do, and you will have fresh, healthy food to eat.

Pull out weeds so plants grow well.

A school garden is good because:

- You learn how to grow fresh food to eat.
- It helps wildlife such as bees and butterflies.
- You can sell plants and **produce** to raise money for other eco projects.

New potatoes

Fresh produce

Lettuce

Eco Hero Activities

Reduce Reuse Recycle!

Here are some ways you can be creative to be an eco hero at school.

Take part in a **campaign** to change something you don't like. You can put up posters, hand out leaflets, or write emails.

Get crafty! Make a bird feeder from reused materials and hang it up in a tree at school.

Hold a "swap meet." Ask everyone to bring small toys and books or magazines to swap at school. The only rule is that if you can't swap it, you must take it home again!

Glossary

campaign   Speak out and take action to change things.

climate change   Harmful changes to our planet and weather caused by pollution.

energy   Something that makes things work, move, or change.

fossil fuel   Materials, such as oil, coal, and natural gas, found deep under the ground that formed millions of years ago from dead animals and plants.

garbage   Things that you throw away that you no longer need or want.

landfill site   A hole in the ground where garbage is buried.

material   Something that is used to make things.

monitor   Someone who checks to see if things are done.

packaging   Bottles, packages, and boxes used to keep food and other products safe and fresh.

pollution   Substance that dirties or poisons air, earth, or water.

precious   Something that has great value because it is rare, expensive, or important.

produce   Food that is grown to be sold.

recyclable   Something made of materials that can be recycled.

recycle   To turn a used material into something new.

reduce   To make less.

reuse   To use something again.

walking bus   A group of adults and children who walk to school together.

waste   Use too much of something especially when there is not very much of it.

Learn More

This book shows you some of the ways you can be an eco hero. But there is plenty more you can do at school to save the planet. Here are some web sites where you can learn more:

www.walktoschool.org/
Find out all about International Walk to School Day and Month and discover events going on all over the United States. Find out about safe routes to walk to school, who's walking, and learn about ways to get involved or launch your own event.

http://www.keepbanderabeautiful.org/aboutus.html
The web site of Keep Earth Beautiful. Take their quiz to find out why we should recycle and to learn more facts.

http://blog.nwf.org/wildlifepromise/2010/11/america-recycles-day-eco-schools-usa-tips/
November 15 is America Recycles Day. This web site informs people when, where, and how to recycle in their community and, in particular, in schools.

www.kidsforsavingearth.org/
A comprehensive and colorful site where you can learn about how kids are saving the Earth, and how you can too.

Note to parents and teachers: Every effort has been made by the Publishers to ensure that these web sites are suitable for children, that they are of the highest educational value, and that they contain no inappropriate or offensive material. However, because of the nature of the Internet, it is impossible to guarantee that the contents of these sites will not be altered. We strongly advise that Internet access is supervised by a responsible adult.

Index